SCHIRMER'S LIBRARY
OF MUSICAL CLASSICS

OTAKAR ŠEVČÍK

Op. 1

School of Violin Technics

Edited by

PHILIPP MITTELL

IN FOUR PARTS

Part I: Exercises in the First Position
Library Vol. 844

Part II: Exercises in the Second to Seventh Positions
Library Vol. 845

Part III: Shifting (Changing the Position)
Library Vol. 846

→ Part IV: Exercises in Double-Stops
Library Vol. 847

G. SCHIRMER, Inc.

DISTRIBUTED BY

HAL•LEONARD®
CORPORATION

7777 W. BLUEMOUND RD. P.O. BOX 13819 MILWAUKEE, WI 53213

Vierter Teil.

Übungen in Doppelgriffen.

Gestossen und gebunden zu üben.

Part Fourth.

Exercises in Double-stops.

Practise both détaché and legato.

1.

Oktaven.

Octaves.

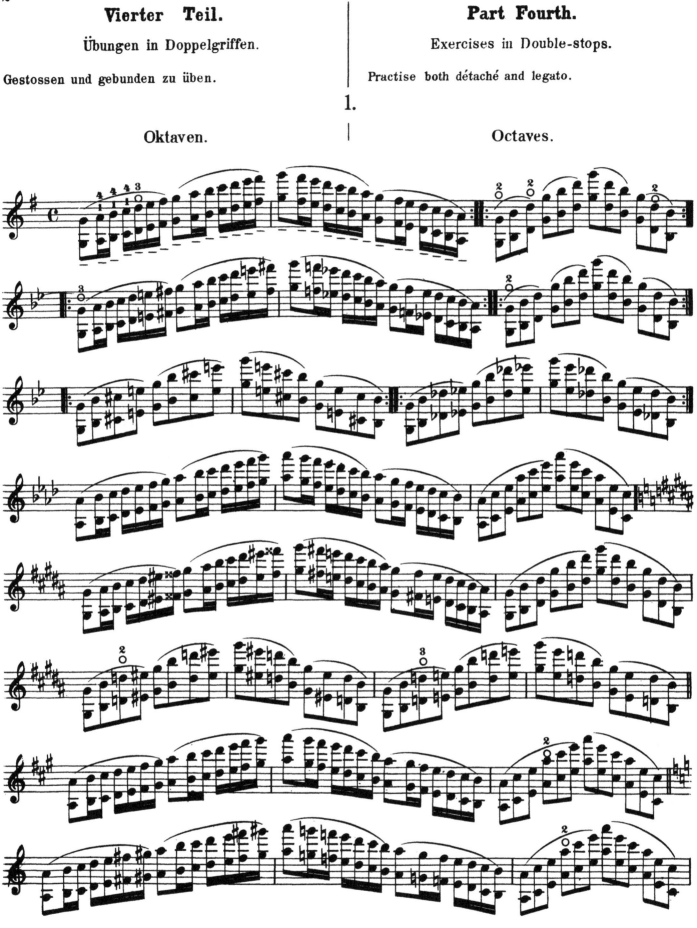

★)Siehe Ersten Teil № 23-26, und Zweiten Teil № 10, 19, 28.

★)See Part First, Nos. 23 to 26, and Part Second, Nos. 10, 19, 28.

17669

Printed in the U. S. A.

2.

5.

Terzen.   Thirds.

6.

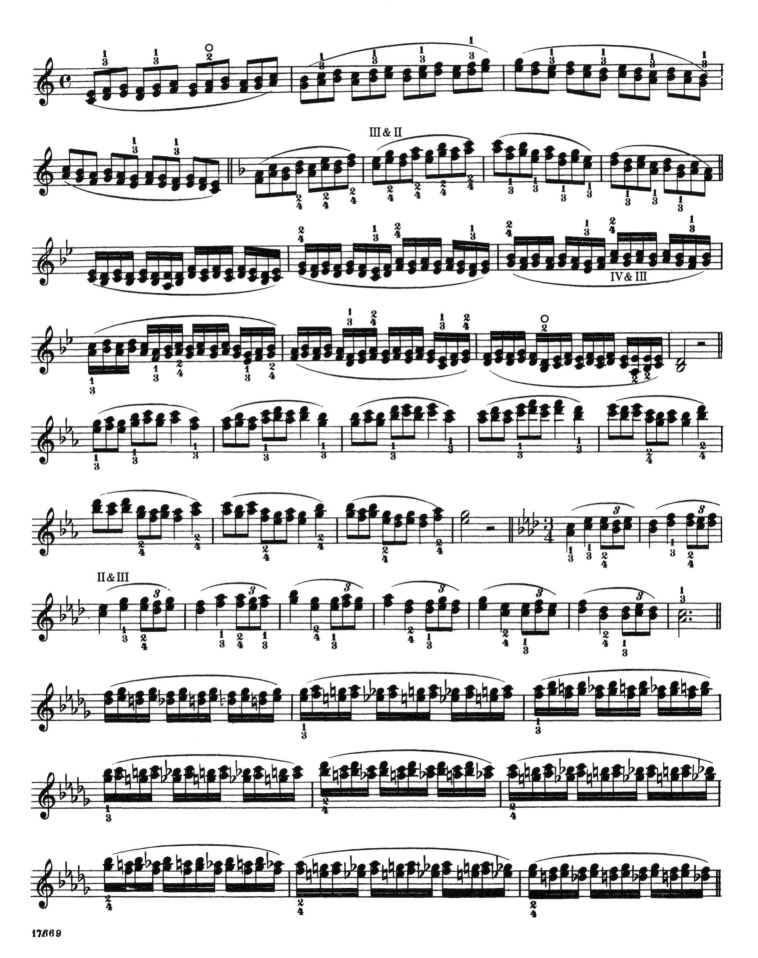

18

7.

17669

8.

9.

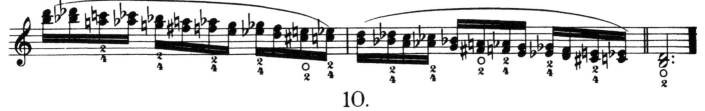

10.

Sexten. | Sixths.

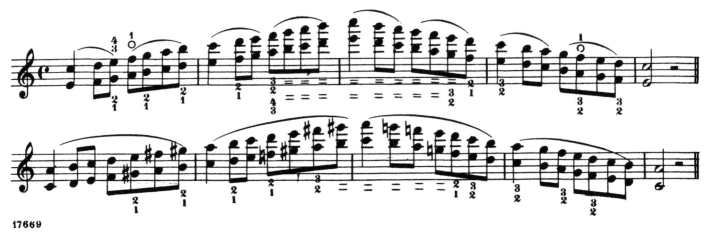

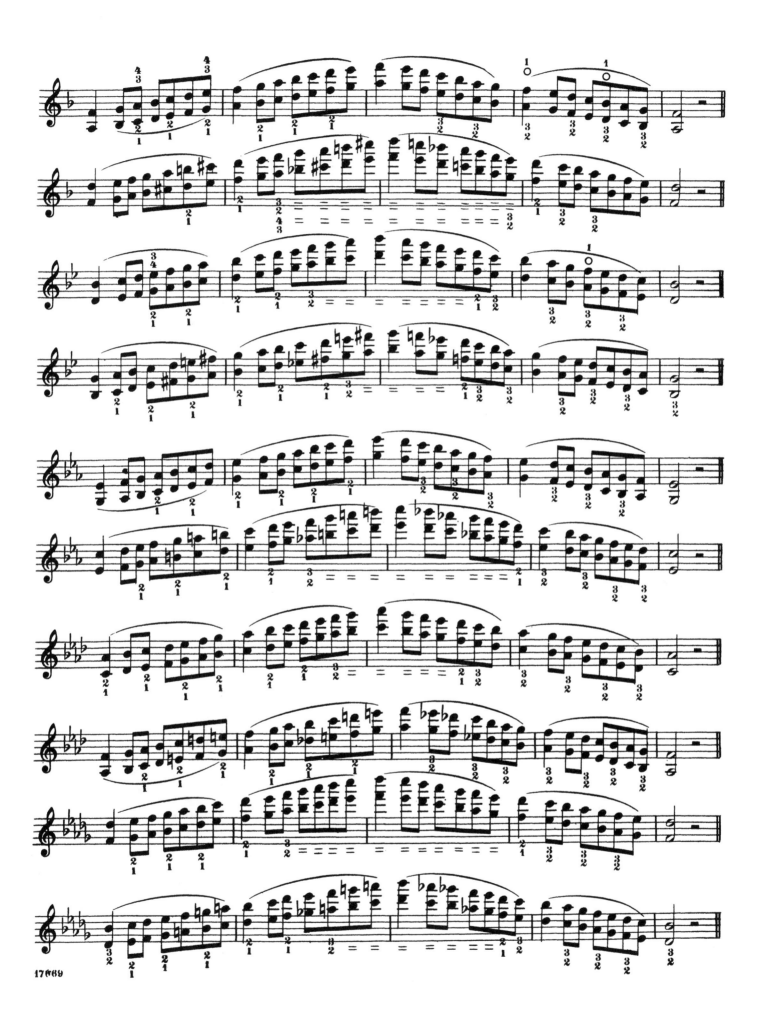

11.

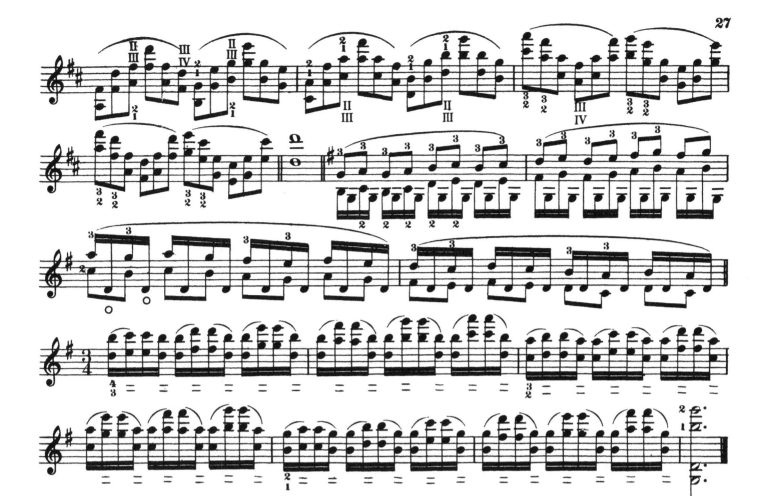

12.

Dezimen.   Tenths.

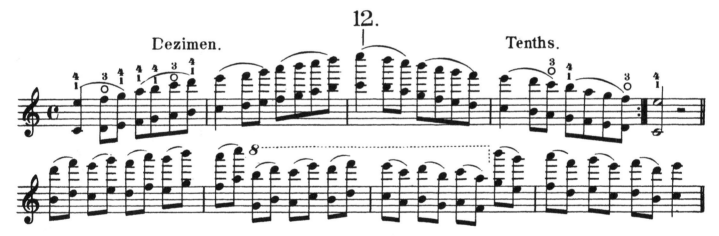

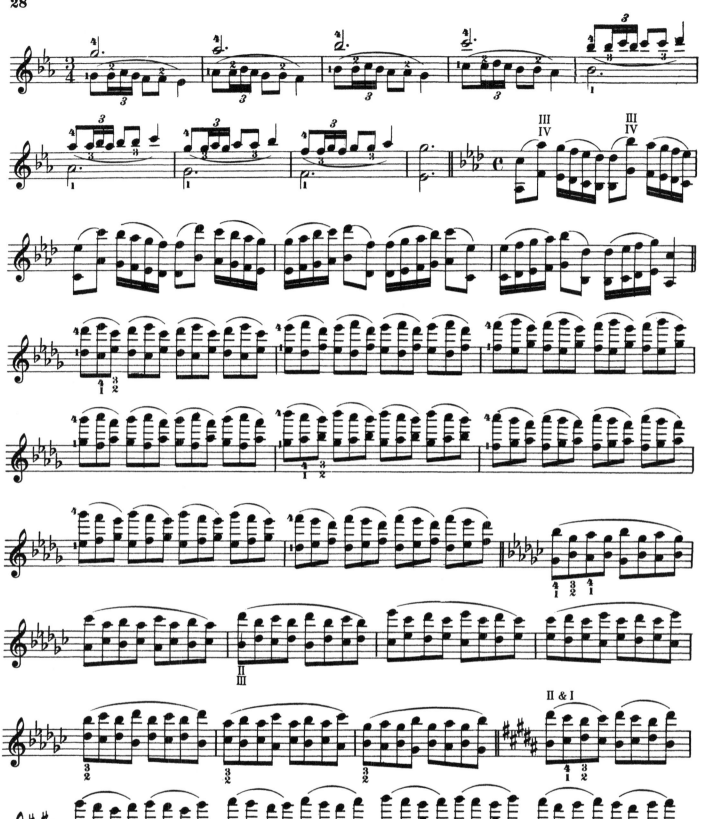

13.

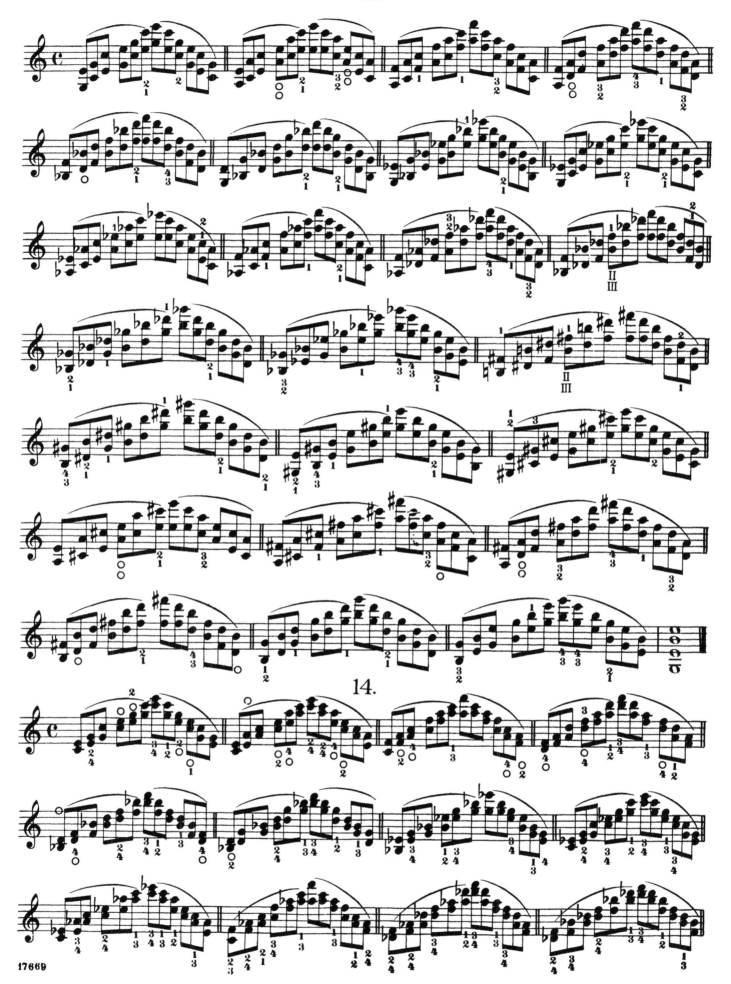

14.

15.

17669

16.

17.

18.

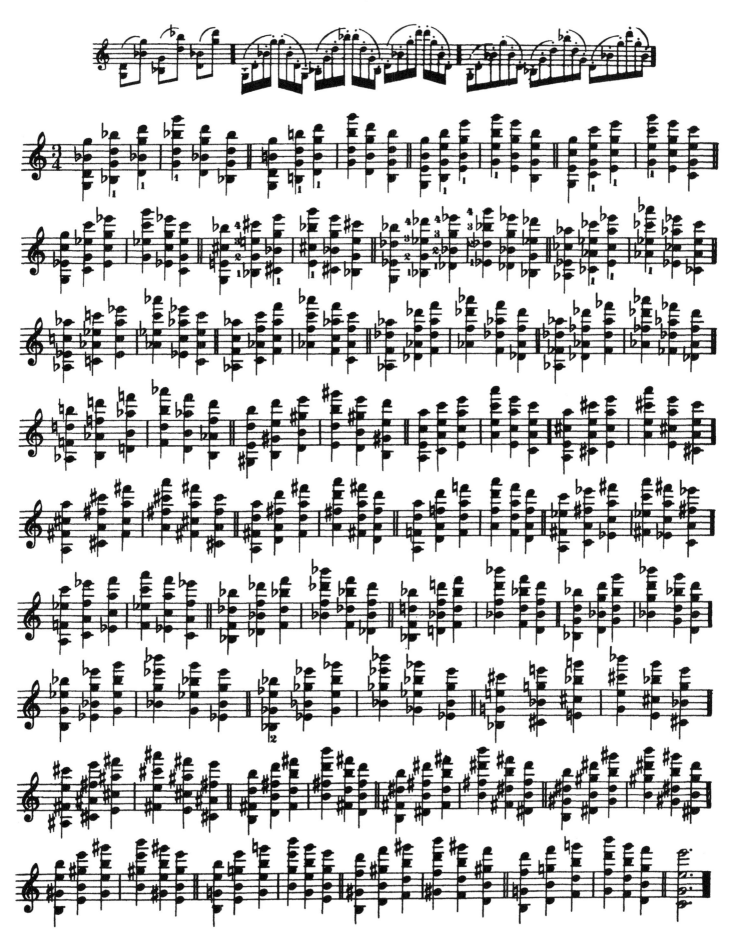

19.

Übungen im Pizzicato
der linken Hand (+).

Exercises on the Pizzicato
for the left hand (+).

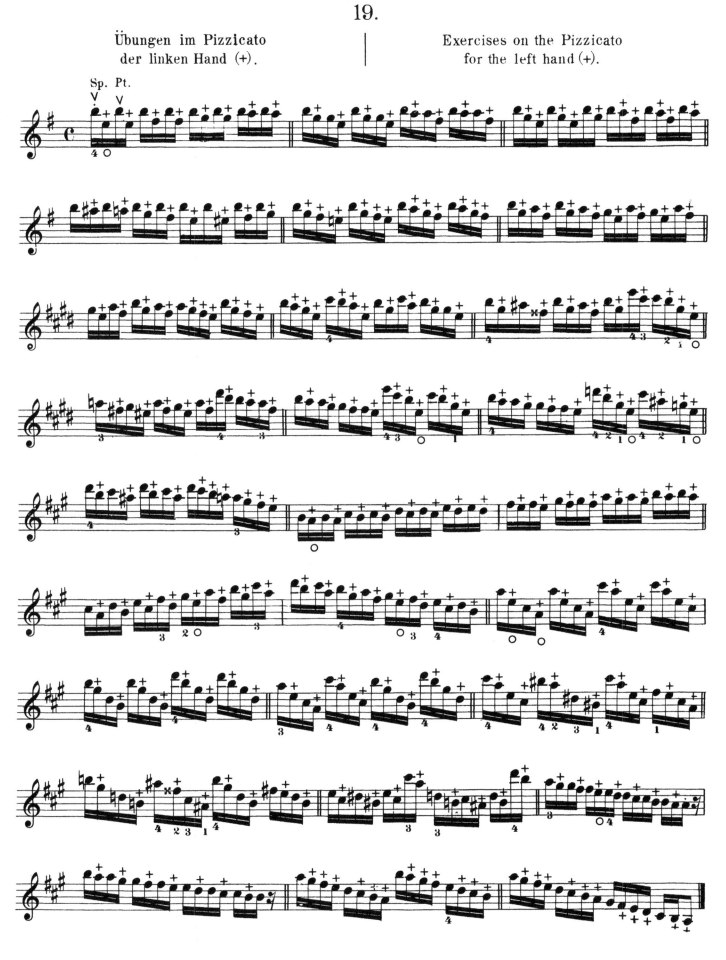

20.

Die Finger, mit denen die Saite gekniffen wird, sind mit römischen Ziffern bezeichnet.

The fingers plucking the strings are indicated by Roman numerals.

40

21.

Übungen in Flageolettönen.

Tonleitern.

Exercises in Harmonics.

Scales.

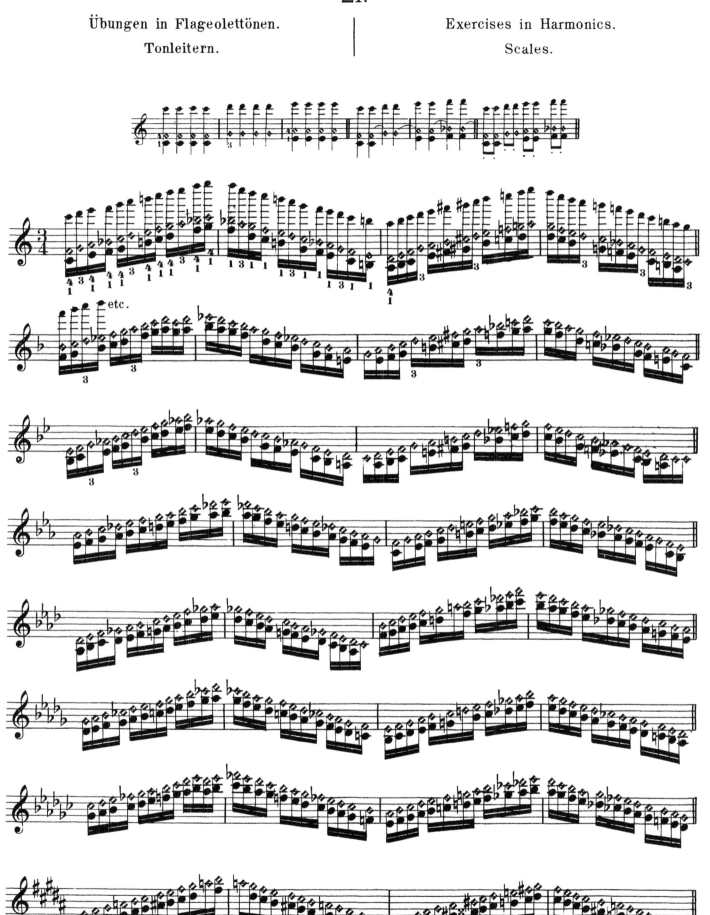

17669

22.

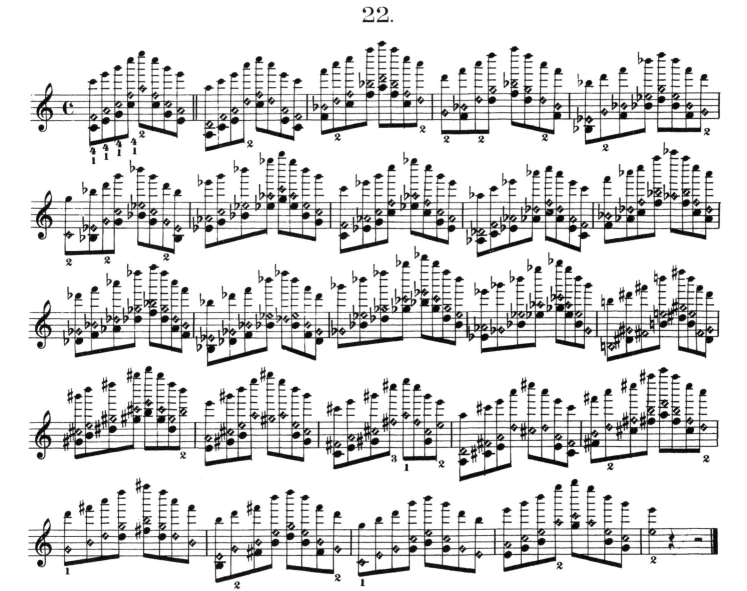

23.

Dur-Tonleitern in Terzen. | Major Scales in Thirds.

In Sexten._In Sixths.

In Oktaven._In Octaves.

Mischungen von natürlichen und Flageolett-Tönen. | Alternation of Harmonics with stops of regular pitch.